Emerging

A Prairie Girl's Journey of Faith

Rita Springer & trudy chiswell

 FriesenPress

Suite 300 - 990 Fort St
Victoria, BC, V8V 3K2
Canada

www.friesenpress.com

Copyright © 2021 by Rita Springer & trudy chiswell
First Edition — 2021

Technical Assistance & Photo Enhancement: Robert Springer
Editing, Typing, Photography: trudy chiswell

All scripture quotes are from The Passion Translation or the
New American Standard bible.

Author contact for Rita Springer: rita@shaw.ca

Front cover painted by Rita Springer

ISBN
978-1-5255-9067-2 (Hardcover)
978-1-5255-9066-5 (Paperback)
978-1-5255-9068-9 (eBook)

1. BIOGRAPHY & AUTOBIOGRAPHY, RELIGIOUS

Distributed to the trade by The Ingram Book Company

Table of Contents

Introduction

It is May 22, 2020, and I am now into ten weeks of isolation from the worldwide COVID 19 pandemic. It's a very different time, and I do believe the world will never go back to what I knew of it before. Living on Thetis Island is much freer than if I was in the city. It is a very quiet island with only 350 people, no shopping, no gas stations, one post office, and a pub. Everyone is observing physical distancing when meeting others, but they do not have to wear masks, be concerned with large crowds, what we are touching, or who we are meeting in the hallways. Life is much the same here as it always has been. I have a great peace in my life—a peace I can only give God the credit for. When I was a child, raised on the farm in Saskatchewan, I had no idea that I would find myself retired on a little island on the West Coast of Canada.

Recently, I had a dream that made me realize how God has protected me over the years from going down different pathways that would have been very destructive to my life and others. Don't we all have questions about what could have been or would have been if circumstances were different? It has been the power of God in my life that gave me the strength to make better choices. I am happy with my current life of freedom and love, and I have no regrets. God's word has guided my life over these many years, trials, and decisions. I started out this walk with God as an assurance to go to Heaven when I died. Now I realize that He is right here with me moment by moment through every thought, desire, and happening. God has always had my back! He has given me incredible confidence in who I am as a woman of God, a wife, a mother, and friend to those He puts in my life.

The Extended Family

So never give up on a friend
or abandon a friend of your father.
*~ **Proverbs 27:10***

My father's family name was Spicer, a name that comes with a long history of ship captains and pioneers. Some of the following stories in this section are from my uncle, Doug Harvey's, extensive research into the Spicer family and the subsequent book he produced on the Spicer Family. Included in my book (with Doug's permission) is only a small portion of his research to give my children a background into their heritage. These roots are where I came from and what made me who I am today.

Captain Eurias Spicer 1846-1926

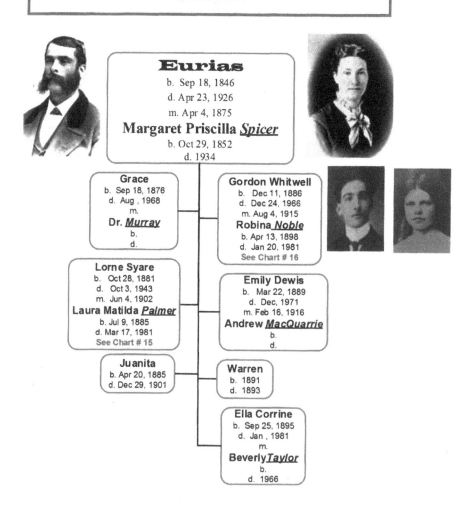

Eurias Spicer / Priscilla (Spicer) Family

Eurias
b. Sep 18, 1846
d. Apr 23, 1926
m. Apr 4, 1875
Margaret Priscilla _Spicer_
b. Oct 29, 1852
d. 1934

Grace
b. Sep 18, 1876
d. Aug , 1968
m.
Dr. _Murray_
b.
d.

Gordon Whitwell
b. Dec 11, 1886
d. Dec 24, 1966
m. Aug 4, 1915
Robina _Noble_
b. Apr 13, 1898
d. Jan 20, 1981
See Chart # 16

Lorne Syare
b. Oct 28, 1881
d. Oct 3, 1943
m. Jun 4, 1902
Laura Matilda _Palmer_
b. Jul 9, 1885
d. Mar 17, 1981
See Chart # 15

Emily Dewis
b. Mar 22, 1889
d. Dec, 1971
m. Feb 16, 1916
Andrew _MacQuarrie_
b.
d.

Juanita
b. Apr 20, 1885
d. Dec 29, 1901

Warren
b. 1891
d. 1893

Ella Corrine
b. Sep 25, 1895
d. Jan , 1981
m.
Beverly _Taylor_
b.
d. 1966

Captain Stephen Spicer 1809-1907

Eurias Spicer 1846-1926   *Margaret Priscilla Spicer 1852-1934*

Captain Eurias Spicer 1846-1926
Written by Doug Harvey

Eurias Spicer, second son of Stephen and Esther (Knowlton) was born in Advocate Harbour, Nova Scotia, Canada in 1846. Advocate Harbour was in the heart of extensive timberland from which businessmen built brigs and brigantines. As he grew up among ship builders and skilled seamen, it was very likely that he went to sea as a young boy. When the opportunity came for him to learn to read and write, he was icebound on a ship in Norway and was twenty years of age.

In 1871, an examination centre and a nautical instructor was available in Canada. Until that time, a sailor was required to write the examination to obtain masters papers in England. At age twenty-five, with many years at sea and a deep knowledge of the use of the ship's instruments, Mercator's Method & logarithms, longitude, latitude, control of disease, and navigation laws, Eurias payed $10.00 to sit for an examination. He received his Master Mariners certificate and was the fourth successful candidate in the Dominion of Canada. Thus began his career in the capacity of Captain. The first ship he commanded was the Wesley Seymour from England to Halifax in 1872; the second voyage was from England to New York in 1872; the third was from Cape Breton to New York in 1874.

In 1875, the year of his marriage to Priscilla, he took command of the J.E. Suthergreen. His first trip was from New York to the United Kingdom. According to the family, his wife often travelled with him, and it's possible some of their children may have been born at sea. Unfortunately, his logbook was lost in a fire, but his trips were many over the years.

Still early in life, Eurias retired from the sea in 1910 with a seafaring record which was, in so many ways, remarkable. Nearly all his passages were good ones. He retired to fully enjoy his comfortable home on Spencer's Island and successfully operated a saw mill and farm. During his life, he owned a car, which to him was more difficult to drive down a country road than to drive the J.E. Suthergreen across the ocean with a "star to steer her by."

Eurias, a stern sea captain, was a loving father, husband, and a community worker. The church was an important part of his life. He laid the hardwood floor in the school that was built in 1884. Eurias insisted his sons and daughters become educated people. Grace, born in 1876, became a doctor; Lorne, born 1881, apprenticed as a shop foreman and then went on to pioneer in the West; Emily, born 1889, became a teacher and later also became a pioneer of the West; Gordon, born 1886, was Rita Lorraine Springer's grandfather who studied business and law and also became a pioneer of the West; the youngest Ella, born 1896, attended finishing school. Gordon's story, handwritten by him, will follow this story.

Life on Spencer's Island (1850-1900) was both gracious and rugged. There were church picnics, bazaars, teas, quilting bees, bathing and boating, with the greatest event of all being the launching of ships. When the Calcutta was launched in 1876, thousands of people gathered from various points in the Bay of Fundy. The ladies of the village set up tea tables and refreshment booths. The proceeds went toward building the church on Spencer's Island. The Calcutta was launched and was a "beautiful exhibit of marine architecture."

Eurias spent his retirement years on Spencer's Island among a close-knit family of Spicer relatives and among his seafaring friends, dying at the age of eighty. Priscilla visited their children pioneering on the Western Prairies as this photo shows.

L-R 1ˢᵗ man – Gordon & Robins Spicer with baby – woman – Priscilla Spicer – 2 women – bottom row 1ˢᵗ child is George Spicer – other children unknown (possibly 1920)

Today in the serene little village of Spencer's Island, scarcely a link remains to recall her gallant age of sail. There is little to indicate that huge wooden vessels were built and launched there, except a few rotten piles on the beach where the shipways stood. Relics of her glorious maritime past are scarce, and models and ship paintings are few. To have turned out so many ships in a little cove tucked away in an arm of the Bay of Fundy is surely a matter that calls for historical records.

∾

Gordon Whitwell Spicer 1886-1966 & Robina (Noble) Spicer 1898-1981

This original story was written by Gordon Spicer at age seventy-two in beautiful longhand, for his children.

I was born in the year 1886 in Nova Scotia at Spencer's Island on the Bay of Fundy: "Where the tide ebbs and flows twice in every twenty-four hours." My parents were Captain and Mrs. Eurias Spicer, and after sailing many seas, father returned from sea and went into the lumbering business, having his own mill. He sawed timbers for the ships built at Spencer's Island and is spoken of in the book, *Wooden Ships and Iron Men* by *Fredrick William Wallace*.

It was at Spencer's Island that I received my public school education, attending Kerr Business College at St. John, New Brunswick during the years of 1906 and 1907, and in the year 1908, I drifted west to Moose Jaw. At that time, the Homestead rage was on, and the Government was supposed to be giving away free Homesteads (160 acres), but it was not so simple to obtain 160 acres. You signed a contract and gave the government $10.00, and they bet the 160 acres of land against your$10.00, wagering that you could not stay on the 160 acres for three years without starving to death. I took them up on their deal, signed the contract, and left for the claim on August 8th, 1908.

Won the bet by a very close margin; even the mosquitoes were on the government's side. The contract called for certain duties to be done—so many acres to be broken each year and a shack to be built. Soon the tractors and threshing machines were with us, and we didn't forget some other things which go along with farming, such as hail, hoppers, worms, and drought. There were no railroad for some years. I hauled grain to Moose Jaw, Viceroy, and Ogema—then we got on the railroad and we were on our way to an easier life.

About this time, I met Robina Noble and we married on August 4th, 1915. Back to the farmstead where we reared a family of 13; seven girls, six boys. Of the girls, there are four teachers, two nurses, one accountant; three boys became farmers and ranchers, one an airman, one an undertaker, and one an accountant.

After raising our family on the farm, Mother and I drifted to Kamloops, BC. With its beautiful climate, friendly people, and rose blooms from June until November. It has been fifty years from that August when I signed the Government claim. *(written in 1958)*

~

Gordon Spicer sitting on old tractors he used many times

Rita's Memories...
Gram Robina & Cousins

My Dad, George Wesley Spicer, was the eldest of the thirteen children of Gordon and Robina Spicer. His youngest brother, my uncle, Lloyd, was only four years older than me, which made an interesting relationship. Lloyd and his brother John were the ones who taught me how to ride their bike on the gravel road outside my grandparent's farm. It was not a girl's bike, but they tied a cushion on the crossbar for me and eventually Mum and Dad bought me a girl's bike. Much time was spent at my grandparent's farm, because my Dad and grandfather worked together. So, rather than call these many young people aunts and uncles, I called them the 'kids' for a long time. My Gram, Robina, was my father's mother and a very special lady. At the age of thirteen, she came over from Scotland with her family as an indentured servant. From my understanding, a family in Winnipeg paid for her ship passage to Canada from Scotland and in return, Robina worked for them for a year while the rest of the family carried on to Mitchellton, Saskatchewan to farm. She joined them on the farm at fourteen when her indentured time was completed. I can remember her sitting on a box at the end of a long closet with my sister, Pat, and

I sitting at her feet. She would take us away to her special place and give us her undivided attention as she listened to our many stories. Can you imagine her giving us her undivided attention with all she had to do with thirteen children? She was my favourite Gram because of how she made me feel so loved during these times. I feel privileged to have received this focused attention, and now I hope I can pass it on to others. We found out after she died that she shared this gift of listening with many other people. Gram Robina was the midwife for the community and delivered most of the children in the area. She was a very strong Scottish woman with a big heart. She even helped raise the farm neighbor's three children when their mother was hospitalized for an extended period. I remember Gram making us doughnuts when we would come over for a visit, and later when I was married, they became a favourite of my husband, Ron, also.

I'm the oldest of forty-three cousins. I remember many gatherings of over fifty people around Gram Robina Spicer's table. Grampa served the meat from his place at the head of the table, with the stack of plates beside him. At Gram's death in 1981, there were seventy-five people linked directly to her. What a legacy she left!

∾

13 children of Gordon & Robina Spicer – George Spicer, (the oldest) at the front of the line

Gordon & Robina Spicer

Gram Robina Spicer's Doughnuts

Robina Spicer

1 cup sour cream *(processed sour cream from the grocery store does not work in this recipe. It must be sour cream right from the farmer)*

1 tsp. baking soda mixed in cream

1 scant cup of sugar

½ cup sweet milk

3 well beaten eggs

¼ tsp. salt

1 tsp. baking powder

¼ tsp. nutmeg

3 ½ cups flour

Mix all ingredients together. Put the mix in the refrigerator to cool before rolling out the mixture and cutting into doughnuts with a doughnut cutter, or as they did in those times, with a glass and a vanilla lid to cut out the hole. Place doughnuts in pre-heated deep fryer and remove when brown.

Gordon Whitwell Spicer / Robina (Noble) Family

Gordon Whitwell
b. Dec 11, 1886
d. Dec 24, 1966
m. Aug 4, 1915
Robina Noble
b. Apr 13, 1898
d. Jan 20, 1981

George Wesley
b. Jan 19, 1917
d. Nov 25, 2002
m. Mar 4, 1941
Edith Edna Woodend
b. Feb 2, 1921
d. Sept. 21, 2014

Ella Mary
b. May 3, 1927
d. Feb. 27, 2011
m. May 7, 1949
Ralph Lenly Pryce
b. Jan 2, 1921
d. May 14, 2006

Evelyn Corona
b. Sep 2, 1918
d. Jul 31, 1965
m. Dec 21, 1941
Kirk Arthur Selanders
b. Jan 2, 1912
d. 1998

Vera Madeline
b. Dec 8, 1928
d. Nov 24, 1997
m. Oct 16, 1954
Samuel Marshall Bruce Willis
b. Feb 8, 1929
d. May 29, 2002

Alice Gertrude Priscilla
b. Jun 17, 1920

m. July 8, 1965
Kenneth Winston Buchanan
b. Apr 27, 1927
d. Dec 24, 1984

Robert Warren
b. Feb 12, 1931

m. Oct 29, 1956
Annie Victoria Mattus
b. Jul 23, 1933

Alice married Robert John Abbott (1920 - 1952) on Oct 20, 1945. After Robert's death she married Earl Laverne Stirling (1917 - 1956) on Jun 29, 1955)

Verna Annie Elizabeth
b. Feb 12, 1933

m. Jun 6, 1956
Donald Wallace Livingstone
b. Oct 1, 1929

Gordon Cecil
b. Apr 14, 1922
d. Jan 10, 2000
m. Apr 14, 1945
Florence Anna May Pingle
b. Sep 16, 1925
d. Feb. 5, 2014

Shirley Mae
b. Dec 31, 1934

m. Jul 9, 1960
Douglas Reginald Harvey
b. Sep 1, 1936

Ruth Mayfield
b. Dec 1, 1923
d. Jul 8, 2001
m. Jun 28, 1946
Leonard Martin McCann
b. Jun 4, 1924

John Alexander
b. Jul 20, 1937
d. May 15, 2011
m. Sep 8, 1961
Thelma Rose Derbyshire
b. Jan 2, 1941

Earl Millard
b. Jul 17, 1925
d. Jan 28, 2010
m. Jun 26, 1953
Christine Mary Martina
b. Feb 9, 1926

Lloyd Whitney
b. Jun 28, 1939

m. Oct 26, 1963
Edna Florence Tompke
b. Jul 18, 1942

Gordon & Robina Spicer family tree

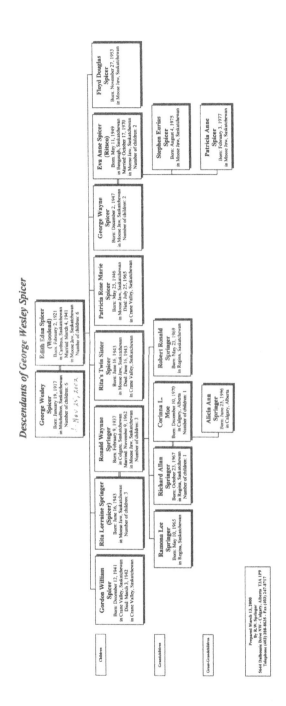

Descendants of George Wesley Spicer

George & Edith Spicer family tree

George & Edith Spicer

George & Edith Spicer wedding March 4, 1941

Spicer Family and the Dust Bowl times of the 30s

The following are excerpts from a school thesis written in 1986 by nineteen year old Laura Livingstone, daughter of Don and Verna (Spicer) after many interviews with Spicer family members. It is included here with Laura's permission.

Grass Roots by Laura Livingstone

My grandmother, Robina Noble, was born in Kineff, Kincardine in Scotland, April 13th, 1898. She and her family immigrated to Canada in 1911. They were part of the "great exodus," when 34,686 people of Scottish origin arrived in Canada in 1911. She was thirteen years old and was paid two dollars per month for her work. One of the farms she worked at was owned by the Reids. It served as a stopover place between Moose Jaw and Davyroyd, and it was here she met Gordon Spicer.

Gordon's homestead was at Section 22, Township 8, Range 28, west of 2nd. In other words, they lived in a small community called

Davyroyd, fifteen miles north-east of Assiniboia. With five dollars to his name, Gordon, who was trying to beat out a rival suitor, set out in his buggy, racing across Lake of Rivers from the Reid ranch to the Noble farm where Robina was staying. Lake of Rivers is a long, thin, and shallow lake in Saskatchewan, and half the time it would be totally dry.

Gordon and Robina were married August 4, 1915. They moved to Gordon's farm and lived in a two-room tar-paper shack until Robina became pregnant. Gordon then built a house consisting of a kitchen, bedroom, and a living/dining room. The home expanded many times in the future. On January 19th, 1917, the first child, George Wesley, was born **(Rita Lorraine (Spicer) Springer's father)** Gordon joked about having a baker's dozen. Little did he realize the irony of his statement, as there were twelve more children born after George.

1929 brought record crops, and the family was doing well, even with eight children at that point. On the farm, a new radio, wind charger, and a new car had been bought. The radio brought entertainment, especially during the thirties. Shows like "Pepper Young's Family" and "The Happy Gang" were coming in loud and clear. While working in the kitchen, Robina would listen to the soap opera of the time, "Ma Perkins," and of course there was "Hockey Night in Canada." The second oldest, Cecil, would always try to have supper early so he could get the cows milked and fed by the time the game started—a process which usually took an hour. When special events were on, the whole neighbourhood came and listened.

The wind charger we bought eventually proved to be just as valuable as the radio. It kept Gordon's batteries, as well as the neighbour's, charged all through the Depression. On the bleakest days, there was always wind, and that meant there was always light, even on the very darkest days.

The crops had been disappointingly small in 1930, and there had been little rain. The farmers were optimistic because they thought it was just one disappointing season to be followed by a good one the following year. The next year, however, was worse. Despite everything, the Saskatchewan Wheat Pool operators continued to talk positively, promising "an initial payment of one dollar per bushel" despite a continuing decline in wheat prices. They were completely wrong. The crop was extremely small; as a result, the pools headed toward receivership and the farmers toward poverty.

When I asked my Uncle George (Rita's Father) about the reason for the crop failure, he did not blame the wind, grasshoppers, or lack of rain. He blamed the severity of the situation on the lack of knowledge regarding crop cultivation and soil maintenance. The thought of summer fallowing seemed ridiculous to the farmers when things were going so well. Obviously, the farmers paid the price for not doing this when they could. The problem of soil erosion became a major concern, and the science of agriculture rose in prominence. Scientists proved that summer fallowing would provide the essential "drift resistant and moisture retaining properties in soil." The disc was a popular mode of cultivating. It would cut the weed and permit the summer fallow to retain moisture but not encourage wind erosion. According to Uncle George, discing was not a solution; it only compounded the situation. The earth was like powder because all the fibre had been removed; using disc only made it finer. When it did rain during the thirties, the water simply ran off the fine dust. Recovery was going to be slow.

Even with a shortage of money, Robina was successfully setting a table for twelve, serving such things as stews, baked frozen fish, and for dessert, Saskatoon berry preserves and rice pudding. The fish were bought in one hundred-pound gunny sacks, which stayed frozen all winter outside. The family went to the St. Augustine United Church regularly. My grandmother would have her nickel twisted in the corner of her hankie, and each child would be given a penny "just to have something to put on the collection plate."

The winter weather during the depression was cold, but no one is really sure how cold it was on the farm because there was no thermometer. The frost on the window was a quarter-inch thick. At night, Gordon would take the ash cans from the stove and put them around the outside of the bedrooms as they gave off some warmth.

If school was cancelled due to a blizzard, there would be a long General Ring on the party-line phone announcing the cancellation. During a long, cold spell, the children would be out of school from the middle of January to the middle of February. To make up for this month, the children would be forced to return from their summer break a month early. During the winter months at school, the first fifteen minutes of class would be spent warming up over the hot air coming from the register.

The dust storms started full force in 1934. It was said that it would pick up without any disturbance and "sweep across the flat fields in a face-pestering stream." My aunt remembers wearing a paper bag on her head so she could breath. There were the years of the terrible dust storms, when you could barely see five feet in front of you. The Russian thistle, which further tried the farmers, were uprooted in these storms and got caught in barbed wire fencing. This would continue until a mess of thistles made up the fence with the dust blowing up against it to form a drift. Many more years passed before these drifts disappeared.

The next three years were the bleakest for the Spicer family. Visits from bill collectors became more frequent and, in 1935, the tractor was repossessed. This was enough to demoralize the proudest farmer. One day, a bill collector was making his way across my grandfather's land knowing full well there was no money to pay the bill. When Gordon and his friend Mitchell saw the bill collector, Mitchell said, "If you don't grab that pitchfork, I will." With the intention of doing no harm, my grandfather chased the bill collector, three-piece suit and all, back to his new 1933 Chevrolet. Although things were bleak, a little humour always alleviated the tension.

In 1937, my grandfather did not sow a single crop, and my grand-mother didn't bother planting a garden either. Just as well, because the average production of wheat in 1937 was 2.6 bushels per acre. They were forced to apply for relief. Churches and welfare organizations in the rest of Canada dispatched thousands of rail cars full of fruit, vegetables, clothing, fuel, and blankets. My grandparents were proud like many other farmers but were thankful that relief in Saskatchewan was considered a loan, preserving self-respect.

Things did get better. The rain came heavily in 1938. The water still ran off a bit but some soaked in, and oh, the prairie-rain smell was heavenly! The farmers started rotating crops and things were looking good, even to the most pessimistic farmer.

When war broke out, the spirits of the farmers could not be broken; bumper crops were plentiful. My grandfather went to court in 1940 as a result of the Debt Adjustment Act and all his debts were cleared. His crop in 1942 yielded sixty-five bushels an acre. He bought two new trucks, a combine and a tractor.

Gordon and Robina Spicer retired to Kamloops, BC in 1958, paying cash for their house. They were secure and, in every aspect, rich: emotionally, with family, and financially. The Dirty Thirties marked a decade of suffering, financial depression and anguish, but those who survived, especially Gordon and Robina with their thirteen children, witnessed accomplishment, perseverance, and courage.

It was a time when a little meant a lot!

It was a time when the main concern of life was survival.

It was certainly a huge test of character to survive under those conditions.

≈

More Pictures From That Era on the Prairies

Gordon Spicer and George Mitchell shared thrashing duties. Below is a picture taken in 1924 of that operation. Gordon Spicer is behind the rear wheel of the tractor and George Mitchell standing by the front wheel.

Lloyd, John, & Rita

One of the few photos with all 13 children. George was engaged and his fiancée Edith is also in this picture.

Rita's Memories of William (Bill) 1881-1972 & Charlotte 1882-1963 Woodend

My mother's parents did many things in their lifetime: farming, market gardening, or working for an electrician while living in a little town called Readlyn, Saskatchewan. Bill Woodend was born in Ulverston, Lancaster, England, joined the 88th Canadian Overseas Battalion in Moose Jaw, August 5th, 1915, and was discharged June 26th, 1918 after being wounded. Grampa Bill Woodend was in the army and stationed in England during the First World War where he met and married Charlotte Ann Balcombe-Colbran. Charlotte was born in Hastings, Sussex, England. Her first husband had been killed previously and she was left with four children when she met Grampa. Grampa was discharged and came back to Canada, followed by Grandma later in February with three children from her first marriage. Imagine what it was like to come to Canada on a ship in the winter and travel across the country on a train only to find your handsome military husband now living in a tar-paper shack with his sister's family. How did they survive the cold, harsh winter, physically and mentally? Grampa had checked on his sister earlier in the winter, before Charlotte arrived, only to find the family burning furniture to keep warm. His solution was to bring them all over to his tiny home to survive until spring. This is what greeted his new bride! My Dad always called Grampa a gentleman farmer. Grampa was a gentle man and always had time for his grandchildren to pick flowers, mushrooms, visit the chickens, or listen to us. My Mum always told the story of how Grampa Woodend always baked pies for Sunday dinner. One day, when Mum was ten years old, he said to her, "That's my last pie to make. Now it's your turn." My Mum loved to bake and became the fabulous baker that we all enjoyed until she moved into assisted living at eighty-two. When we visited, Grandma Woodend always served high tea around 4:30 p.m. Sometimes, sister Pat and I would be sent to the store for a brick of Neapolitan ice-cream—a special treat.

Grampa & Grandma Woodend

Furness Woodend   *Grampa Woodend*

Descendants of Henry Balcombe

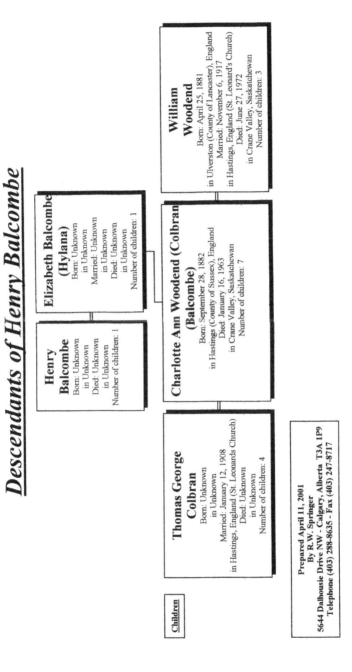

Children

Henry Balcombe
Born: Unknown
in Unknown
Died: Unknown
in Unknown
Number of children: 1

Elizabeth Balcombe (Hylana)
Born: Unknown
in Unknown
Married: Unknown
in Unknown
Died: Unknown
in Unknown
Number of children: 1

William Woodend
Born: April 25, 1881
in Ulverston (County of Lancaster), England
Married: November 6, 1917
in Hastings, England (St. Leonard's Church)
Died: June 27, 1972
in Crane Valley, Saskatchewan
Number of children: 3

Charlotte Ann Woodend (Colbran) (Balcombe)
Born: September 28, 1882
in Hastings (County of Sussex), England
Died: January 16, 1963
in Crane Valley, Saskatchewan
Number of children: 7

Thomas George Colbran
Born: Unknown
in Unknown
Married: January 12, 1908
in Hastings, England (St. Leonards Church)
Died: Unknown
in Unknown
Number of children: 4

Prepared April 11, 2001
By R.W. Springer
5644 Dalhousie Drive NW - Calgary, Alberta T3A 1P9
Telephone (403) 288-8635 - Fax (403) 247-8717

The Farmer's Daughter... not the Farmer

You even formed every bone in my body when you created me in the secret place, carefully, skillfully shaping me from nothing to something. You saw who you created me to be before I became me!
~ Psalm 139: 15-16a

I grew up on a farm in Southern Saskatchewan. I was the oldest of four: a sister, Pat, and two brothers, Wayne and Floyd. It was a very easy time. Dad had a couple of sections of land or about thirteen hundred acres. The farmhouse was a story and half of basic wood-frame construction. Originally, it was a simple tar paper shack that they'd moved to a foundation and added on to. Years later, when my husband Ron went to move something in the old section of the house, he found the insulation was horse hair in the walls. Mum used to tell the story of how the one wall in the tar paper shack was not permanent, and if you wanted to make the living room bigger, you just moved the wall. Downstairs, in the new home, was a kitchen, living room, and two bedrooms, with two more bedrooms upstairs. The kitchen was the biggest room downstairs with the kitchen table serving as the gathering place for all events. Friends, family, and farm workers would all be gathered around that table. The coffee pot was always on with Mum's freshly baked goods on the table. If you didn't get dressed by 8:00 a.m., you wouldn't get dressed until noon because the coffee and talk were always flowing. There was a large cook stove on one wall and no refrigerator or ice box, as we didn't get electricity until 1953, and ice was not delivered way out in the country. Anything needing to be kept cold in the summer, like the butter, was kept in a pail down the well. In the winter, things were just kept outside in one of the buildings. It was a warm farm kitchen and everyone was welcome.

We got a refrigerator, which sat in one corner of the kitchen until the power got hooked up a month later. I remember the day I saw deep holes being dug along the side of the gravel road outside the house, and then long poles were slid into them. Then, the linemen strung wire on the poles for the electricity to run into the house. My Dad and a friend, who was an electrician, scrambled around in the attic running wires from the connection to all the rooms in the house. They had to feed the wire between the two by fours, through the horse hair insulation, and fish it out through the switch boxes with a coat hanger. It was quite a process.

There was no water or bathroom in the house. A pail of water had to be carried up the hill from the pump to the house for everything. Saturday night was bath night in the round galvanized tub put in front of the oil burner in the living room, and water had to be heated on the cook stove. We each took turns washing with the youngest going first and Mum and Dad going last. In the winter, clothes would be draped over a chair in front of the oil burner so they would be warm in the morning when we dressed for school. No bathroom in the house meant running to the outhouse or using the chamber pot under the bed in winter. Never mind the rolls of toilet paper horded for the pandemic; we had to use the old Eaton's catalogue pages for wiping. Mum had a wringer washing machine that had a gas motor in it. All the clothes and bed sheets, during both winter and summer, were hung outside on lines to dry. In winter, they froze solid, and you would have to bring them into the basement to finish drying. All farmers' wives believed this was the way to do it during both summer or winter. They loved the fresh air smell of the cloths and the sun-bleached whites.

~

Life on the Farm

Life on the Farm

Life on the Farm

Wayne & Floyd Spicer with Chocolate the horse

Grama & Grampa Spicer's farm home

Life on the Farm

Rita, Lloyd & Pat Spicer

Edith Spicer with the children doing chores: L-R Pat, Wayne & Rita

Life on the Farm

Rita with Baby Floyd, Pat & Wayne 1953

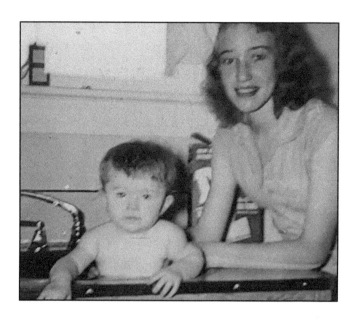

Rita bathing cousin Robin

Life on the Farm

4H Beef Calf Achievement Day

4H Dress Review (Rita's preferred)

4H and Life on the Farm

*Then He will give you rain for the seed which you will
sow in the ground, and bread from the yield of the
ground, and it will be rich and plenteous; on that day
your livestock will graze in a roomy pasture.*
~ Isaiah 30:23

There was a small, red barn on the property where the animals were kept. One milking cow for our own use, a riding horse and, of course, the barn kittens were kept there. We were never allowed to make pets of the animals because they were either sold or butchered and eaten. But we always had a dog and many cats. It was always a game to find where the mother cat hid her new kittens. Sometimes, we would find them in the hay bales, the old car, under the granary, and one time in the attic. One evening, when we were sitting in the living room, we could hear very quiet mewing. The search was on! In the attic we found four wee bundles of fluff in an old box of clothes. We realized the attic door had been left open and mother cat had found that the box of old clothes was the best place to birth her kittens. When she went out for food, someone closed the door and she was locked out. Momma cat was finally reunited with her babies and moved to the barn. You never knew where you would find new surprises. I loved to collect things; big toads, kittens, and bunnies were my friends. My Mum was never sure what would jump out of the drawers or my pockets.

Outside, Dad had a herd of about 150 red and white Hereford cows to sell and use for our own meat. In the early years, there was a group called 'the beef ring' that had a special building on our property to slaughter beef for the personal consumption of the community. There was no refrigeration at that time and no ice box, so in the summer months, one family would bring their cow to slaughter. After it was done, the family that brought the cow would get the best cut, and the remainder would be distributed to the rest of the community. I think that in the winter, a family could slaughter a whole cow for their family consumption because they could freeze it in one of their out-buildings as temperatures plunged to 15 degrees Fahrenheit or -9 Celsius.

Dad grew wheat, barley and oats on the farm. At harvest time a hired man would come to help, but as the two boys got older, they would help Dad bring in the harvest. This was stored in six granaries on the property or taken and sold to the red grain elevators near the railway tracks that crisscrossed Saskatchewan at the time. This was then distributed across Canada by rail boxcars. Now the railway track in that area is pulled up, the grain elevators are gone, and trucks are used to haul away the harvest.

When I was ten years old, I tried farming in 4H with a beef calf. The emblem of 4H stands for "head to clear thinking, heart to greater loyalty, hands to larger service, and health to better living." It was started in Roland, Manitoba in 1913 and was a roaring success. School authorities, parents, and the agriculture industry revered this simple idea that sparked the 4H movement.

Part of my responsibility was caring for the calf by cleaning his stall, feeding, watering, grooming, training him to lead with a halter, and to stand properly for the show. Everything had been going well and my little steer was growing and responding to my training. In early spring I was ready to show him off to the family. Between the barn and the house was a large body of muddy water called the slew, created from the spring thaw and the winter run-off from the barn. So,

you can imagine what was in that water! All was well as I led my calf around the slew, put him through his training skills, and had our picture taken. But then disaster hit! My cute little calf decided enough was enough. Off he took for the barn at a dead run, right through the muddy, smelly slew with me still holding on to his lead rope. Not a pretty sight! I was covered from head to toe in slew mud and water. So much for my farming days, and hence my long-time statement became, "I'm the farmer's daughter, not the farmer." I did find joy in 4H home craft which included sewing, embroidery, dress making, knitting, creating record books, and my most enjoyable subject: leadership training. Achievement Day was the highlight of the year when everyone's work was on display to be judged. What an accomplishment!

Mum had Floyd when I was ten years old, and since she loved to garden, as soon as I got home from school, I was given the job of looking after baby Floyd so Mum could go out in her garden. On many occasions when I got home from school, Mum would say, "Rita, bake a cake for dinner." I would respond, "Ok, where is the recipe?" "Don't worry," she said, "I'll just tell you," and off she would go to sew something in the bedroom. I don't know how I ever learned to cook because Mum never used a measuring cup or measuring spoons, but her cooking was always delicious. Now I use both of those measuring tools and stick to the recipes of Mum's that finally got written down.

A highlight of harvest was going with Mum to take dinner out to the fields. The stew, in a big pot, was put in a box with the everyday dishes from the kitchen, cutlery, homemade bread and butter, and the cake of the day. Everything was carried out to the field for the workers' lunch in the farm truck. Machinery and noise would temporarily stop, and workers would gather around for Mum to serve them. They'd sit anywhere they could find a comfortable spot on the ground to eat. It was a busy time, but for us kids it was an exciting and rewarding time to see the results of all of Dad and Mum's hard work. During harvest time, my job was to help Mum in the kitchen preparing the meals for the workers. I never worked out in the fields like my friends. I was not the farmer; I was the farmer's daughter. I remember Mum whipping up these two recipes many times during the harvest to take out to the field with the pot of stew.

~

Edith Spicer's Chocolate Cake

Edith Spicer

2 cups flour

1 ½ cup white sugar

½ cup cocoa

¼ tsp. cream of tartar

1 ¼ tsp. baking soda

¼ tsp salt

Mix the above dry ingredients and then add the following ingredients.

1 ¼ cup of milk

2 eggs

½ cup lard

1 tsp. vanilla

Mix all ingredients together, and then bake in oven at 350 for 30 minutes in a 9x13 inch pan.

Edith Spicer's Rhubarb Thirst Quencher

5 lbs. of rhubarb cut in pieces (3 – 3 ½ cups per pound)

2 slices of lemon

1 $^{1/3}$ cups of honey or 2 cups of sugar

Put the above ingredients in a pot and then cover with boiling water (about 3 quarts). Let stand for 24 hours, stirring occasionally and then strain and chill. It is then ready to serve.

NOTE: The process may be hurried along by bringing all the ingredients to a boil

∾

The One-Room School House & school in the winter

Train up a child in the way he should go,
even when he is old, he will not depart from it.
~ Proverbs 22:6

I attended a one room school house for two years. There were grades one through three and then two people in grade nine. I have been told that today there are only two active one-room school houses in all of Canada. One is here on Thetis Island where I live. Miss Blanch Gates, the teacher, boarded at our house, and the two of us would walk the half mile to school together in the nice weather. In the winter, my Dad would hitch up the horse to the cutter, and we would pile into it with lots of blankets to ward off the freezing weather. He would drive us across the pasture to the small, white-frame school house. There was an oil-burner stove in the middle of the room and the teacher's first job before the students arrived was to get the stove burning to warm up the freezing classroom. My job was to clean the black-board at the front of the room while the teacher was lighting the fire. Of course, we had to keep our coats on until the room warmed up. Oil burning stoves were necessary on the Prairies because there were no trees around to cut down. I always said, "If you saw a tree on the Prairies, there was a little farmhouse near-by, or there had been at one time."

Having the school teacher live with you had its good and bad points. She would help me with my homework, but she also reminded me of my homework. After two years at the little, white school house, things changed. We had to go three miles on a bus to a school in the town of Crane Valley and still had to walk half a mile in good weather to where the bus picked us up. But, in the winter, a Bombardier snow coach picked us up at the farmhouse door and drove across the fields of hard-packed snow. It was yellow, just like the school bus, and it had benches inside with little round windows on either side of the vehicle. Everyone brought a blanket to keep warm on the trip. There were skis on the front and tracks on the wheels to go over the bumpy fields or anything it encountered, looking very much like a tank used in the war. This was the pre-curser to the snowmobile. There were always changes coming; some good and some not so good, but changes nonetheless. The question was: how did I handle the change, or was I willing to change? Riding to school in this manner went on with the Bombardier for a few years until the roads got better, and there was snow removal equipment.

I grew up in a very peaceful way of life, relaxed with no pressure. My beautiful collie dog was named Collie. Very original! We could send her for the milk cow, and she would bring the cow home to the barn for milking.

Mum and Dad raised us with very good morals. You looked after one another, respected your neighbors, and didn't do anything bad. Well, most of the time! Mum and Dad were good people, but we never attended church. When I was ten years old, I asked Santa Clause for a bible. Now, I can't tell you why at ten years old I would ask for a bible, but I did, and I received it. Initially, I tried to read it, but I didn't get very far before it was put on the shelf to collect dust. I just didn't understand the words or have anyone to guide me through it. I think God was drawing me to Him at that young age, even though I didn't realize it at the time.

Bombardier Snow Coach

Rita in Grade 5 (find her)

Rita in High School

Meeting the Love of My Life

*Let every wife be supportive and tenderly devoted to her husband, for this is a beautiful illustration of our devotion to Christ. Let every husband be filled with cherishing love for his wife and never be insensitive towards her. ~ **Colossians. 3:18***

Rita & Ron

Weyburn Sask.
Box 482.
April 11, 1962.

Dearest Rita:

I had hoped to write before this but hope that you will pardon the delay. It is not because I haven't been thinking of you darling as you have been constantly in my thoughts. It seems that this week has gone even slower than last week but I am sure that it makes us appreciate our week ends together that much more.

Lloyd tells me that he never saw Marilyn over the week-end until he picked her up to bring her back. I am sure that he was disappointed with the way things turned out but that is his problem, not mine.

There is not much news since I last saw you except to tell you that Rod and I finally managed to see a hockey game on TV last night (Ha Ha) I am sure that you and Marilyn will appreciate that.

I will be leaving Weyburn after dinner on Saturday and will meet you at your place when you get off work. I hope that this week-end

[2]

does not fly by as quickly as last weekend did. I have so many things to say to you honey but I will leave them until I see you Saturday.

Love

Ron

R. L. BAMFORD & CO.
CHARTERED ACCOUNTANTS
AT POINT OF MAILING

5 CANADA

Miss Rita Spicer,
2356 Rose Street,
Regina, Sask.

In 1962, at the age of nineteen, I married Ron Springer, and we began fifty years of life together. April 1st, 1962, I was invited by my Uncle Lloyd to go to a house party in Weyburn. Upon arriving, I passed a young man leaving to take his date home. He returned a few minutes later and was introduced as Chick Springer. My comment was, "Your Mother must have given you a better name than that." He then introduced himself as Ron Springer. Everyone in Weyburn, including nieces and nephews, called him Chick. Ron drove me home to my uncle's new apartment that night and then on to my apartment in Regina the next day. We continued dating and were engaged on my birthday, on June 16th, 1962. Not a bad April fool's joke after all!

Ron grew up on a farm in Colgate, Saskatchewan until he was four years old, when the family moved to the small city of Weyburn. Born February 9, 1937, Ron grew to be a tall man of six feet and four inches. He was kind, generous, full of good humor and a great story teller with an optimistic perspective of life. His generous nature, however, is perhaps the most endearing of his qualities. It afforded him many friends as he always tried his best to help someone in need. Always having the ability to size up a situation and seize the opportunities as they came along, he looked for endeavors with more gain and less pain. Graduating in 1954 as valedictorian of his class, Ron went on to be the first student to graduate in Saskatchewan as a chartered accountant through a correspondence program. He then became a leader and entrepreneur as an accountant.

The big night arrived when I was going to meet Ron's folks, Cleo and Stan North, and stay over for the weekend. Driving to Ralph, Saskatchewan, Ron said, "Don't be surprised if the whole clan is there. I asked Mom not to tell anyone but if she told my grandmother, everyone will know you are coming and want to meet you." As we pulled up to the remodeled, old brick schoolhouse, sure enough there was hardly room in the driveway to park the car. Walking into the kitchen, we found twenty some people; Ron's Grandmother, Aunts, Uncles, Nieces and Nephews—all gathered around the kitchen table playing cards or in the living room, waiting for us to arrive. Everyone was very welcoming except Ron's nine-year-old niece. At one point when we were sitting on the sofa, she came up to me and announced, "He is MY Uncle Chick!"

Ron's Mom was a great Mother-in-law! None of the stereotypes about Mother-in-laws fit her. She was always an encourager. We baked together, sometimes making twenty-two dozen doughnuts for the freezer. Mom North taught me how to crochet my first tiny sweater set when I was carrying our first child, Ramona. She taught me how to make her famous shortcakes, and I continue to make them to this day. They were Ron's favourite.

Merv & Ron Springer on the farm in Colgate

Ron Springer's family. L-R Cleo, Merv, Clarence & Ron in back

Mom North's Shortcakes

Mom North

2 cups flour

2 tsp. baking powder

½ cup shortening
(butter or margarine) COLD

½ cup sugar

Pinch of salt

¾ cup milk

Rub the first five ingredients like pie pastry, then mix in the milk. Roll out 1 ½ inch thick and cut into biscuits; be sure they are touching in the pan. Sprinkle with sugar. Bake at 425°F for 15 minutes.

Mom North's Hot Chocolate Mix

6 cups Carnation instant milk

1 cup powdered sugar

1 small 16 oz. or 3 cups Nestles Quick

16 oz. or 2 cups Coffee Mate

Mix above ingredient well. Serve 3 tsp. in each cup with hot water.

Mom North's Puffed Wheat Cake

½ cup butter or margarine

½ cup corn syrup

1 cup brown sugar

2 Tbsp. cocoa

1 tsp. vanilla

8 cups puffed wheat

Put all of the ingredients except the puffed wheat in a saucepan and mix together. Bring to a rolling boil, and boil for 1 minute and 30 seconds. Then, pour the hot mixture over the puffed wheat and mix thoroughly together. Spread evenly in a greased 8-inch cake pan and let cool. Cut and serve. Enjoy!

One night when we lived in Regina, Mom and Stan dropped in on their way through the city from a holiday in BC. I had been sick for a couple of days and with three pre-schoolers running around, the house was a disaster with dishes piled up in the kitchen. Oh my, what she must have thought! Mom North took one look around and said, "Stan, you and Ron go bring in the dishwasher from the car, and we will get the dishes done." It was a portable dish washer that her sister-in-law had given her in BC. Mom thought maybe I was in more need of it than she was. What a blessing! I sure appreciated it for many years to come.

We had a great relationship with Mom and Stan North. Stan, Ron's step-father, was wonderful to Ron and they did many renova-

Mom & Stan North

tions together. Both were six foot four inches and could hang ceiling drywall without a ladder. Ron felt that their marriage, which happened a year before Ron's and mine, was the best thing that happened to his mother.

Wedding bells rang for us in the Zion United church on November 9th, 1962. We began married life in Weyburn, with many of the same dreams and ambitions as other couples: raising a family, creating a home, and developing a strong social network. Winters for Ron and his friends in Weyburn consisted of evenings filled with bridge, and Ron tried to teach me to be his bridge partner. I never liked the game and it was a wonder we stayed married. The best thing that happened was that we moved to Regina in the spring.

Ron & Rita get married November 9, 1962

Starting a Family

Let all the little children come to me and never hinder
them! Don't you know that God's kingdom realm exists
for such as these? Listen to the truth I speak: whoever does
not open their arms to receive God's kingdom like
a teachable child will never enter it.
~ Mark 10: 14-15

1960 was the decade of babies in the Springer household. Initially, there was heartbreak over three lost babies to miscarriage. Love, Peace and Patience were the lost babies' names. The loss did not devastate or destroy our devotion to one another and our desire to have a family. Ron was working as a chartered accountant at the government Income Tax office. In 1965 with the help of a little stitch, (the first in Regina) a bundle of joy named Ramona Lee was born to our family, although a few weeks earlier than she was due. Now this changed everything! It was a mutual agreement between Ron and I from the beginning that I would stay home and keep the home front stable. I finally felt fulfilled with my little family. Sadly, two more miscarriages followed; Rose Marie and Rebecca Anne, so we decided to enlarge our family through adoption. In 1968 we welcomed Richard Allan, a four-month-old little boy with red hair. As he grew, Richard looked so much like my brother Wayne that everyone thought he was our biological child.

The 5 Rs

Ron-Rita & Ramona 1965

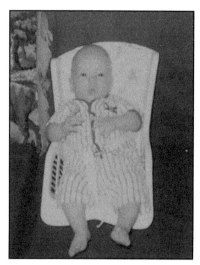

Richard 1967

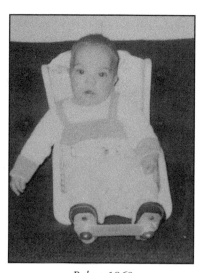

Robert 1969

In 1969, as we were preparing for holidays, we got a call that three-month-old Robert Ronald, our next bundle of joy, was ready to come home into the mix. We then became the 5 R's: Ron, Rita, Ramona, Richard, and Robert. Robert had many surgeries before coming home because of a problem with club feet and wore special boots with a bar between them. But we were still going on holidays, and so how we would manage a wee baby in the car was considered. I searched all over Regina for a baby basket to no avail and finally had to settle on a dog basket that would sit on the front seat between Ron and I for the baby. Today, my son Rob still jokes about how the dog basket was the root of all his problems. When Ron and I first married, we planned to have two children and adopt one, but God changed that to one biological child and two chosen boys. All my joy!

Raising three children was not always easy and had its ups and downs, but I really would not change it. My career was raising my family with involvement in many volunteer activities, and I thoroughly enjoyed it all. As with my Mum, I enjoyed baking for my family. These were some of my family's favourites:

≈

Rita's Matrimonial Squares

1 ½ cups rolled oats

1 ½ cups sifted all-purpose flour

1 tsp. Baking Soda

1 cup Brown sugar (packed)

1 tsp. salt

¾ cup shortening

Date Filling

2 cups of dates

1 cup of water

1 Tbsp. lemon juice

½ cup Brown sugar

Cook above ingredients in a saucepan. Stir and cook until thick. Cool and then pour over bottom layer of crumble in the pan.

Heat oven to 350°F and then blend dry ingredients. Add shortening and rub together with a fork, then use your fingers to make a crumble mixture. Press ½ of the mixture firmly into greased 9x13x2 inch pan. Spread cooled date filling on top of the mixture. Sprinkle remaining crumble mixture on top and pat lightly. Bake 25 to 30 minutes or until golden-brown.

Rita's Best Date Bran Muffins

1 ½ cups bran

1 cup whole wheat flour

2 ½ tsp. baking powder

½ tsp. baking soda

½ tsp. salt

¼ cup brown sugar

½ tsp. cinnamon

¾ cup chopped dates

1 egg

3 Tbsp. molasses

1/3 cup oil

1 ½ cups milk

Pre-heat oven to 400°F. Mix dry ingredients together and add dates. Mix egg, molasses and oil together and beat in the milk. Pour liquid mixture into dry ingredients and stir to moisten (don't overmix or batter will be runny.) Pour into muffin pans and bake at 400°F for 15 minutes.

The 5Rs family

The growing 5Rs

Richard, Ramona & Robert

Rita & Ron Springer

25th Wedding Anniversary

Meeting Jesus

For it is by grace you have been saved, through faith
and that not of yourself, it is the gift of God
*~ **Ephesians 2:8***

Forty-eight years ago, in 1972, I invited Jesus Christ into my life to be my Savior and Lord. At the time, I had no idea how it would impact my life.

In the spring of 1972, I was in North Dakota, when I met Jane, who lived down the street from me. Jane was not an evangelist, but she became my good friend. We would have coffee and chat as our children played together. I baked a lot then, and I could swear Jane could smell the cinnamon buns when they came out of the oven. She always arrived at my back door for coffee.

One day, Jane invited me to go to a Christian women's luncheon with her. I felt a bit intimidated by the word Christian, since I knew I wasn't right with God, but I didn't know what to do about it. It was a delightful afternoon; the lunch was excellent, they had a fashion show, and it was a fun time.

Then a lady got up to speak and told us how Jesus Christ helped her so much in her life. She said God wanted a relationship with us, but that we were all sinners and we fell short of the glory of God. Now I did not believe I was a sinner! I lived a decent life; I had not killed anyone nor had I stolen anything. I was a good person! She explained that my sin separated me from God. Then she talked about how all the good works in my life would never remove my sin; only Jesus could do that. Jesus paid the price for my sin when He died on the cross and rose again to eternal life. Eternal life? What is eternal life? She said that everyone who trusts in Jesus Christ alone has eternal life, and that life begins now and lasts forever. Wow! I knew I wanted whatever this woman had, but I had no idea what this would mean in my life.

She went on to say that Jesus helped her with her attitude towards her children and how to respond to her husband. I knew that I could do with some help in those areas of my life. Ron worked eighteen hours a day, and I had three pre-school children at home—all day, every day. What Mum doesn't need help? She said Jesus would help me with all my frustrations—if only I would let Him.

At the end of her talk, she explained that all we needed to do to be right with God was to pray with her. So, as she led everyone in the prayer of accepting Jesus Christ as their Savior, I prayed with her. Later, she invited those who had prayed with her to let her know. She gave me a little booklet to explain what I had done that day. My friend, Jane, was there for me and suggested that we start a bible study in her home. What a friend! I still didn't believe I was a sinful person, and it took many months of bible study before I realized that I really was a sinner, because I missed the mark of God's perfection. I was always comparing my goodness against other people, not against God's perfection. After reading about my grandparents and great grandparents, I realized that I came from a long line of God-fearing people, so it was no wonder that God drew me into a relationship with Him.

The next week, we started a bible study in Jane's home with four other women, and the babysitter looked after all the children at my home. Over the next four months, as we read and asked questions about the bible, I gradually learned how to walk with Jesus on a daily basis. Things were not perfect after that, and there were many stormy times, but Jesus gave me the strength to cope with the challenges that come with raising a family. Jesus became my strength from that day onward.

When we moved back to Calgary, Jane called ahead to get me connected to another Christian women's group and bible study. They held monthly meetings for Christian women of all denominations who would come to hear testimonial speakers, eat a very scrumptious lunch, and be entertained with a special feature of the month. For many years, I was involved with different aspects of Christian women's clubs, from bible study to administration and organization. Over the years, I became a speaker, traveled around Alberta to different Christian women's clubs, held various positions at all levels of council, and became the Regional Representative for Southern Alberta. Through this, my faith grew. My faith gave me the strength and peace throughout the most difficult times. It has made me stronger and enhanced a sense of compassion for others.

How did I learn to trust God in these situations? I was blessed with a special friend in Peggy Christensen, who guided me on my walk with God. I met Peggy at Christian Women's Club in Calgary and, over the years, we became fast friends. She used to say we were the twins, even though Peggy was a petite, tiny woman, and I was five foot seven. Ten years after I became a believer, I was able to travel with Peggy when she was speaking for Christian Women's Club. I witness her spending hours with Jesus in the early morning, and how she used it to direct her daily life. She definitely was a great encouragement to me on how to start my day, and inspired me in get to know who Jesus is before rushing into the day. I also realized that things went so much better when I had spent time with Him before starting the day. It has continued to be a part of my daily life all these years, and I'm so thankful for Peggy's friendship and what she taught me.

Peggy Christensen & Rita at Christian Women's Club

Peggy Christensen a very dear friend over the years

I could openly share my strong faith in Jesus in various women's groups, but for some reason, I had difficulty verbalizing it in my home. We went to church and the children went to Sunday School, but they never made that commitment to my Jesus the way I did. I realize now that the church we had chosen didn't teach about a personal relationship to Jesus. It is my greatest sadness now that I didn't get the message across to my children when they were young, how accepting Jesus as their Saviour could change their life in a positive way. When my oldest son was an adult, he came to faith in Jesus, but he went through many trials before that.

I read in a book that everyone needed a prayer partner, so I asked God to show me who that should be. I felt God should choose them. One day at a Christian Women's meeting in my home, I felt God was showing me that Gladys was the lady to be my prayer partner. I really wasn't sure, but I asked her anyway. Gladys says she said she would pray about it, but from my perspective it seemed that she had said no. I was confused and questioned if I heard God right. I continued to pray. Two

Gladys Kern & Rita at Capernwray

weeks later, Gladys approached me and said that if I was still willing, she was interested in being my prayer partner. We have been prayer partners for over forty years, praying for one another, our families, and our concerns. A prayer partner does not need to know all the event details; they just need to pray and lift their partner up to God, trusting Him for the outcome. Through our connection in prayer over the years, Gladys and I became as sisters.

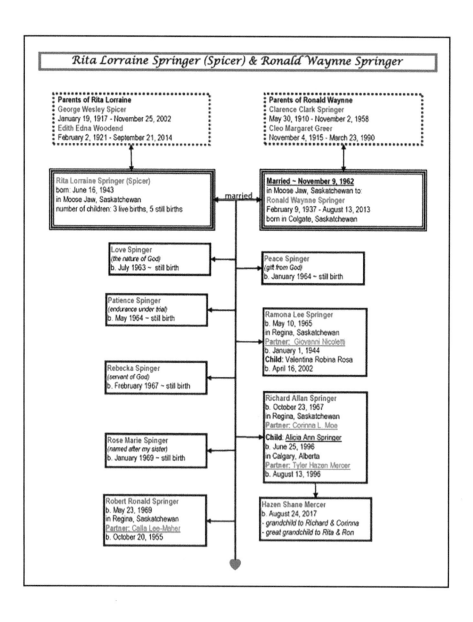

Rita Lorraine Springer (Spicer) & Ronald Waynne Springer

Parents of Rita Lorraine
George Wesley Spicer
January 19, 1917 - November 25, 2002
Edith Edna Woodend
February 2, 1921 - September 21, 2014

Parents of Ronald Waynne
Clarence Clark Springer
May 30, 1910 - November 2, 1958
Cleo Margaret Greer
November 4, 1915 - March 23, 1990

Rita Lorraine Springer (Spicer)
born: June 16, 1943
in Moose Jaw, Saskatchewan
number of children: 3 live births, 5 still births

married

Married ~ November 9, 1962
in Moose Jaw, Saskatchewan to:
Ronald Waynne Springer
February 9, 1937 - August 13, 2013
born in Colgate, Saskatchewan

Love Spinger
(the nature of God)
b. July 1963 ~ still birth

Peace Spinger
(gift from God)
b. January 1964 ~ still birth

Patience Spinger
(endurance under trial)
b. May 1964 ~ still birth

Ramona Lee Springer
b. May 10, 1965
in Regina, Saskatchewan
Partner: Giovanni Nicoletti
b. January 1, 1944
Child: Valentina Robina Rosa
b. April 16, 2002

Rebecka Spinger
(servant of God)
b. Frebruary 1967 ~ still birth

Richard Allan Springer
b. October 23, 1967
in Regina, Saskatchewan
Partner: Corinna L. Moe
Child: Alicia Ann Springer
b. June 25, 1996
in Calgary, Alberta
Partner: Tyler Hazen Mercer
b. August 13, 1996

Rose Marie Spinger
(named after my sister)
b. January 1969 ~ still birth

Robert Ronald Springer
b. May 23, 1969
in Regina, Saskatchewan
Partner: Calla Lee-Maher
b. October 20, 1955

Hazen Shane Mercer
b. August 24, 2017
- grandchild to Richard & Corinna
- great grandchild to Rita & Ron

The 5 R's...
Ron, Rita, Ramona, Richard & Robert

Children are God's love-gift; they are heaven's generous reward. Children born to a young couple will one day rise to protect and provide for their parents. Happy will be the couple who has many of them!
~ Psalm 127:3-5

I am blessed to be the mother of our children, Ramona, Richard, and Robert, as well as grandmother of Alicia and Valentina, and now great-grandmother of Alicia's child Hazen. I am a blessed woman! I am thankful for all that I have experienced in life.

I saw God's hand in my daughter's life when she was choosing a life partner who I didn't feel was a good choice for her. Feeling the situation was out of my control, I had to leave it to God to work out and felt I was to pray for Ramona rather than say anything. One day her fiancé approached me and said, "You have to talk to her. She has asked for a week to think about our life together." All I said to him was, "Give her the week and wait." Then a funny thing happened during the week. The hotel where we had booked a room for the reception called and asked if we still wanted the room, as they had another request. After sharing this with Ramona on the phone, I was thankful when she said, "Let it go, the wedding is off." Wow! I saw God's response, His love, and God's faithfulness to Ramona as the details unfolded to release her from a difficult situation, which would have affected her life in a negative way. I prayed, asking God to open her eyes. Now, Ramona has a good life partner with Giovanni and has given me a beautiful granddaughter, Valentina, to spoil. Ramona became a tailor with her training, and now her and Giovanni have their own tailor shop.

I had the privilege of being with Ramona in the delivery room when my sweet granddaughter was born. It was such a special experience because I had a C-section with Ramona and was out cold for the whole thing. When Valentina was two, Ramona went back to work in the tailor shop, and we enjoyed having Valentina every Saturday until she was twelve. She loved to make cookies or sit on Ron's knee to play with him on the computer. When Grandpa Ron got tired of entertaining her, he would say, "Go see what Gramma is doing." Ramona was very particular about what Valentina would eat, and she always arrived with her little lunch. But when lunch arrived, Valentina would say, "I'll have the same sandwich that grandpa is having" which would have been white bread with bologna and cheese. Not what Mom sent! So, Gramma would eat Valentina's lunch and Valentina would have what Grandpa was having.

≈

Giovanni, Ramona & Valentina Nicoletti

Valentina Nicoletti

One morning, at 4:00 a.m. in 1986, I answered the door to find a policewoman who asked if I knew where my son was. I knew Richard was smoking pot and questioned if that was why the policewoman was at my door. He said it made him feel good and that he could stop any time he wanted. "Nothing wrong with smoking pot, it should be legal" he claimed. But he spent a few months in jail because of it.

Have you ever had a huge metal door slammed and locked behind you? Behind that huge metal door of the jail was my fourteen-year-old son, Richard. Emotions were high! I held it together while visiting him on my own, but as I slid into the front seat of the car, I was a blubbering mess. It was pouring rain outside and the tears ran down my face. As I looked down there was three inches of water at my feet from a previous hole in the fender. There had been an accident and the damage hadn't been repaired properly. What a mess I was in all the way home; water outside, my feet in water, and tears streaming down my face as I drove the sixty minutes home. The only thing I felt God saying to me as I drove was, **"strength"**. So, upon arriving home, I looked up the word strength in my bible.

But the Lord stood with me and strengthened me,
so that through me the proclamation might be fully
*accomplished. ~ **II Timothy 4:17***

It was September 7th, 1986. Yes, God has strengthened me as I continued to walk with Him, depending on Him step by step for guidance in raising Richard. It was a difficult time, and there was nothing I could do but entrust Richard to God's hands. There were many ups and downs over the years, but God always gave me strength and wisdom in how to react. At times, I found myself being controlled by Richard's mood swings when he lived at home. Within ten minutes after he got home, I would be in the same frame of mind that he was.

I did not want to be controlled by a fourteen-year-old, so I prayed, asking God to change me, and He did. I no longer responded to

Richard's mood swings. I don't know how God does these things, but I do know that only He can do it. Without God I could not have survived the worry.

One day, years later, I came **home** to a message from Richard on my phone: "Mum, I have fallen in love with Jesus." WOW!

It blew me away to hear that Richard had given his life over to Jesus. God and Charles Stanley have been his teachers these past few years. Some days he is very frustrated, but he continues to hang on to Jesus and read the Word. Only God can do these things in our lives. I had surrendered Richard to God, kept praying, and waited to see what God was going to do. I had no idea what that might be or when, nor did I know what Richard might do, but all I could do was entrust him to God's hands. Richard has asked me how I knew that I could trust God with him. I had to! I could not run every time he threatened suicide.

What followed were many years of daily phone calls and long chats. I listened to his anger, frustration, hurt, and yes, his suicidal thoughts. I would pray and call out to God for His help for Richard. I realized that even if I was sitting in Richards's living room, I could not prevent him from doing something stupid. We lived about two hours away from one another. I knew that all I could do was commit him into Gods care and trust that God was looking after the situation. It was such a privilege to listen to him, his concerns, and discuss what he was reading. He had difficulty with reading as a child, and yet now he was a voracious reader and able to quote things from memory. I have been blessed to see the results of God's work in Richard's life. I feel He has him in a serene place, teaching him the path that is right for him. Today, I still have long talks on the phone with Richard, and he shares what God is teaching him. As a mother, it is good to see him growing. His life has turned around and he has a lovely home in the country that gives him lots of pleasure and room to do the things he wants to do. Setting up a pressure washing business has given him the freedom to follow his own path in life. Richard has also been reunited with his adult daughter, Alicia, who gave him his first grandson, Hazen. Such a joy—my first great-grandchild!

~

Rita with 1ˢᵗ grandchild Alicia

Richard & Alicia 1996

Richard's farm

Richard doing what he loves to do

It has been 48 years since I surrendered my life to Jesus, and He has slowly been guiding and leading my life all these years. It still amazes me that God loved me so much that He sent His only Son to die for my sin, so that I could have a relationship with Him.

For God so loved the world, that He gave His only begotten Son, that whoever believes in Him shall not perish, but have eternal life. ~ **John 3:16**

One day in 1991, my other son, Rob, called me to say, "Mum, I'm going to Victoria for a couple of weeks to see if I really like scuba diving." Rob got interested in diving and developed a love for the ocean in Hawaii, and this transformed into a life-long love of diving in BC. The magnesium company he had been working for in High River had closed its doors, so he felt he would go for a holiday. Robert liked the west coast so much that he never came back to Calgary except for a visit. Being my youngest child, I knew I needed to let go of him also. He advanced to acquiring a Dive Master certificate, teaching diving and underwater photography, and has become a very accomplished photographer and graphic designer in the process. Rob went to college in Victoria for photography and then graphic design in Nanaimo. You never know where life will lead you; you only need to be willing to take a chance sometimes. Rob only dives for pleasure now while enjoying the beautiful west coast waters and scenery. I now have the privilege of getting to know him and his partner Calla as adults. They continue to look after me in such a special way, and we enjoy each other's company since my moving to British Columbia in 2014. God gave me the courage to let go and release my youngest child to His care. It wasn't easy to let Rob go, but I was getting more practised in trusting God to give me strength and courage with life's curve balls over the years.

Rob Springer & Calla Lee-Maher

Rob & Calla

Swimming with the dolphins

Rob underwater about 12 years old

Life had its ups and downs, but it was also sometimes a "wait and see what was around the next corner" type of situation. God didn't promise me a rose garden, but He promised to always be with me. He always had a way of sorting out a situation that was different than I expected it to be. At one-point, my husband, Ron, was going to the casino quite a bit, and I was concerned. I prayed and asked God's help to show him that he could lose a lot of money. All of a sudden, he quit going. When I asked why, Ron told me that instead of losing a lot of money, he had made a great deal. I never asked how much, but it scared him to the point that he knew he could also have lost a great deal. God can turn our lives around in such different ways. We just have to keep our eyes open to see what He is doing for and in us day by day.

~

Losing the Love of my Life

For the true widow is all alone and
has placed her complete hope in God.
~ I Tim. 5:5

Ron Springer

In September of 2011, Ron, my husband, was diagnosed with pulmonary fibrosis. His life went downhill very quickly, losing eighty pounds and needing ten liters of oxygen a minute to breath. Over the two year course of his illness, I saw him go from a very big man to a very sick man in the span of a few months. He passed away on August 13th, 2013. God chose not to heal Ron like I would have liked, but he went before the disease got so bad that he would have had to go into a nursing home. He would not have done well in a nursing home, and so I praise God for His love for us both in taking him sooner. The love of my life, since I was eighteen, was now gone after fifty years of married life. While I grieved over the previous two years of his illness, I was thankful that Ron didn't have to experience the debilitating effects of the disease. We had a good life through the ups and downs, and I thank God that I have no regrets. Ron's illness was totally out of my control, but God gave me the strength I needed during that time to care for Ron and face tomorrow without him.

What Now...
Bible School at Seventy-One?

The Lord looks down in love, bending over heaven's
balcony, looking over all of Adam's sons and daughters.
He's looking to see if there is anyone who acts wisely, any
who are searching for God and wanting to please him.
~ Psalm 14:2

My whole life had been involved with raising my family and looking after my husband, Ron, but now what was I going to do now that I was on my own and with all the children raised?

For three years, my friend Gladys and her whole family had gone to a bible camp on a small island in British Columbia during the summer. I asked her to bring me back some information about it. Bible school had never been on my bucket list, so I don't know why I asked for information, but I did. Gladys brought back the brochures and a few days later I called the office at Capernwray Harbour Bible Centre on Thetis Island, BC. Rachel, the admission secretary, suggested I come for five days and check out the place with an introductory program called Taste and See. I would be immersed in the student body and see what they were doing each day. I signed up for the five-day adventure. When I told my friend Peggy about it, her response was, "I am going with you to check it out and make sure you aren't getting involved in a cult."

On April 9th, 2014, Peggy's husband, Lawrence, and my son, Rob, drove us to Chemainus, British Columbia and helped us load all our suitcases on the little ferry heading across Stuart Channel for Thetis Island. We were on a new adventure. Peggy is a petite woman of less than five feet, but she had two huge suitcases because she said she didn't know what she would need. I had one suitcase, but I was concerned about how we were going to get off the ferry with three big suitcases, let alone walk to the property of Capernwray. We must have looked like we were permanently moving in with all our luggage! I thought at the time, "What am I getting myself into?" As we started coming into the Thetis Island dock, two young women asked if we were going to Capernwray. We said yes, we were, and they offered to take our luggage for us. Thank you God! An answer to prayer. The girls were students at Capernwray and exemplified the hospitality and welcome we received during our five days there. The next five days we experienced a joy and delight in this beautiful place perched on the edge of Thetis Island and the Stuart Channel. There was a peace about the place, acceptance, and a feeling of being right at home. At the end of our time, Peggy was thrilled about the place and I decided to sign up for the September 2014 school year.

Capernwray Harbour Bible Centre, Thetis Island, BC

What a change my life was about to take. I was about to launch into school with about one hundred young people at seventy-one years old. What would it be like? Could I do this? School had always been difficult for me, and I had to question if I was up to it or if it was a foolish move.

My Mum, at ninety-three, was in a nursing home at the time, but she was such an encouragement to me to go for it. In fact, the last time I saw Mum, she said to me, "Haven't you gone yet?" It seemed she was waiting for me to get settled in the next chapter of my life. Even my children were encouraging me to strike out on this new adventure.

Initially, I thought I was just going to lock the door of the house and walk away for a year while I went to bible school, but in June 2014, I felt God saying to me to, "Get out." So immediately I put the house up for sale. My daughter, Ramona, said to me, "Mum, you can't expect to get rid of all the contents and sell the house in two months." God said it, I believed it, and it happened with the help of friends and family. On September 15th 2014, I left the keys on the counter, Robert and I left for BC, and later in the day the new owners took possession of the house. I was on my way! September 2014, a year after Ron passed away, I got rid of my home and all its contents and went to Capernwray Bible School on Thetis Island, BC for two years. Capernwray is a bible school located on beautiful ocean front property, bordering the Stuart Channel on one side and the Strait of Georgia that goes between Vancouver Island and the mainland of British Columbia on the other side of the island. The only way to get to the island is either by ferry from Chemainus on Vancouver Island or the float plane that leaves from Vancouver. It is an evangelical Christian post-secondary institution that was founded forty-one years ago by Charlie and Marlene Fordham as part of the world-wide organization of Torchbearers International. There moto is, "Training of men and women to be equipped for full-time Christian service, regardless of their occupation." They also have a ministry to older Christians who just want to spend time in God's word to deepen their faith journey.

Classroom at Capernwray

Rita, Rosalinde & trudy outside the Victoria Legislature

Meeting Rainbow Rose

Who would go to bible school at seventy-one years old with one hundred students all much younger than myself? Most of the students were under twenty or in their early twenties. It was a great experience. Everyone had a forty-five-minute chore each day. You will never guess what mine was! I was washing pails of eggs every day and stacking them in flats to go in the refrigerator. Mum would sure chuckle because I always said I was the farmer's daughter, not the farmer. Anything to do with the farm was not my idea of fun. We had lectures every morning and evening from a book of the bible. It was very exciting to discover Jesus in the Old Testament as well as the New Testament.

For many years, I have always questioned why God would wipe out a whole group of people. But as we studied the Old Testament, I realized that He had tried again and again to get their attention. They would not listen and continued to act selfishly and ignore God. I ponder how often I have done the same thing. There was a time in my life when I didn't even recognize that I was resisting God the same as the Israelites had done.

I was only in school for two days when I got word that Mum had passed away and had to leave for the funeral. My brother, Floyd, had not been well for years and sadly in January of 2015, he also passed away. Losing more loved ones was hard, but Capernwray was a good place for me to be. It was a place of healing and letting go: letting go of Ron, our home, Mum, Floyd, and all our "stuff" that had accumulated over fifty years of marriage.

On Sundays, we were encouraged to go from Thetis Island to Vancouver Island for church. We were encouraged to check out some of the churches on the list and then settle on one church as our main congregation. I chose a church in Nanaimo to get connected to for the year. After church, Rob and Calla would pick me up, and we would have lunch and spend the afternoon catching up. Then, they would drive me back to Chemainus so I could catch the 5:10 p.m. ferry back to Thetis Island and Capernwray for another week of school. I would arrive back just in time for the special Sunday night dinner. Everyone dressed up, with the ladies always wearing skirts or dresses and the guys in dress pants and ties. The evening service was always a wonderful time of worship and sharing what we'd learned or what God had done in our lives that week.

One day in November of 2014, the admission secretary, Rachel, asked me if I would host a new lady coming for Taste and See for five days. As I came down the stairs that Sunday afternoon, I saw a lady sitting at the table where I normally sat. I went over and introduced myself and met trudy. There was an immediate connection that we both felt and, over long talks, we found many things in common. For one, we had both just sold our homes and their contents, and we were both technically homeless and looking for direction for the next chapter of our lives. Quite a thing to be homeless at seventy-one, but for all the right reasons!

When trudy's five days of Taste and See were finished, she invited me to stay at the apartment she was renting on Dallas Road in Victoria for the four-day February break from school. Another student and I drove down to Victoria, and we enjoyed walking around the city, seeing the legislature, Fisherman's Warf, and Inner harbour. One evening, when walking down around Inner Harbour, we heard a little voice singing in the night. Out of the darkness came a petit woman dressed in a skirt with a poufy crinoline under it, and an arrangement of balloons on her head. We started chatting with her and found out that she was living in a women's shelter after having a car accident and losing everything. She made money performing as a clown for children's birthday parties. After she showed us her multi-coloured crinoline, we dubbed her 'Rainbow Rose' from that point on. We gave her a little change that we had, and that was my first experience of being able to share my faith with a homeless person.

Israel Trip

In January I was mulling over what I was going to do with two weeks off for the March 2015 spring break. Capernwray offered various mission trips and a trip to Israel for two weeks. I was torn between a desire to go on the Israel trip and going home to Saskatchewan to spend some time with my brother, Floyd, as he was not well. When Floyd passed away January 6, the day before we needed to sign up for Israel, I felt God giving me the okay to go on this adventure, but I had concerns. At seventy-one, was I physically up to the challenge? I approached Chris Fordham and asked if he thought I could handle the walking that was involved, and he encouraged me to go for it.

The trip from Vancouver to Israel was a very long overnight flight. Sitting in the middle seat, one man on one side would fall asleep and then the one on the other side. I was not able to sleep on a plane sandwiched between two men I didn't know. We finally arrived in Tel Aviv in the early morning and went straight on a tour. What an awesome opportunity to be a part of a group of students, alumni, and staff of Capernwray, and to walk where Jesus walked.

We saw all the tourist sites, one being the Dead Sea. The Dead Sea is a salt lake bordered by Jordan to the east and Israel and the West

Bank to the west. Its main tributary is the Jordan River. The reason it is so salty is that in the dessert, the water evaporates more quickly than water in the open ocean. This is the deepest, saltiest lake in the world. It is nine times as salty as the ocean, which makes swimming more like floating. I waded out into the water and through the gooey mud with the help of two of the girls. Laying back to float and enjoy the water seemed like the natural thing to do. All was well until I tried to stand up in the water and couldn't get my feet to go down to the bottom. Help! The water was so salty that I had to get the help of the girls to stand me upright. I felt like a beached whale, so out of control.

One afternoon, we went to the Mahane Yehuda market in old Jerusalem. I have never seen so much food! Square blocks with stalls of fruit, nuts, goodies, and tourist items like carvings of olive wood, scarves, religious icons, and anything you could imagine. People, people everywhere! The market was very crowded with vendors noisily and aggressively hawking their wares, and people trying to barter for a lower price.

We traveled on a big tour bus. Narrow streets meant holding our breath every time we had to pass another vehicle on the road. When the bus stopped at a site, there were usually another twelve other tour buses parked, which meant there were crowds of people to maneuver around everywhere you went.

The highlight of my trip was the two of nights we stayed in a little, four-story hotel in Old Jerusalem. We woke up in the morning to see the shop owners putting their patio tables and chairs on the street for people to enjoy a morning coffee on their way to work. Very quaint! We were also able to tour the new Holocaust museum in Jerusalem. The museum was a very emotional and sobering experience. Our two-week visit to Israel was a very well organized and thought-provoking trip. Then, we headed back to Canada for the final semester of school.

Scenes of Israel

Scenes of Israel

Scenes of Israel

Upon arriving home, I said to my brother, Wayne, "You haven't seen rocky land until you go to Israel. You may have picked rocks yearly on the farm in Saskatchewan, but Israel is covered with rock everywhere. If you see a patch of grass by the side of the road, there will probably be a shepherd grazing his goats and sheep. There isn't much grassland there as it is a very dry dessert landscape."

The end of my first year at Capernwray culminated with a lovely commencement ceremony during the first week of May. The weather was perfect: the sun was shining, pink cherry blossoms lined the drive-

way, giving the property a festive flair. It was a great accomplishment to finish the year, and it had been a long time since I walked across a stage for gradua- tion. Staff worked very hard for a whole week, preparing delicious food for the buffet dinner. Food was served in big, white tents on the lawn and patio where family and friends gath- ered. There was much excitement, but also sorrow as we were leaving one another after an intense year together. Many hugs, many promises to keep in touch, and lots of fond farewells.

At the end of the day, we all boarded the ferry, dragging all our belongings or loading them into the waiting cars to go home. There was only one problem. I was homeless, as my granddaughter Valentina reminded me later that summer. School was over for four months. The year at Capernwray had been amazing, but I really felt I could benefit by repeating it again without the distraction that two family deaths had created. I registered to come back the following September for a second year and was accepted. I wasn't ready yet to make another permanent home decision. When I told Valentina about my deci- sion over the phone, she very quickly said she was sending out a new resume. I asked her, "What are you sending out a new resume for?" Her response was, "I'm sending out for a new Gramma because you won't be here if you are going back to school for another year." She was not happy!

Ramona and Giovanni graciously invited me to stay with them for the summer. My time with Ramona, Giovanni, and Valentina was a very special. I enjoyed their hospitality and got to know Nelson, Valentina's one-year-old puggle dog. One day, he had me pinned on the couch and I needed to call for help in order to get him off my chest. He is now very respectful when Gramma comes to visit.

Summer...
The End of the Farm

*This will provide a beautiful foundation for their lives
and secure for them a great future, as they lay their hands
on the meaning of true life.* ~ **I Tim 6:19**

First, we had to settle my brother Floyd's farm before it was put up for sale. Off I went to spend a month on the farm, sorting and disposing of not only Floyd's possession, but what remained when my parents left the farm twenty-six years ago. My brother, Floyd, never married and had no children to inherit the farm, so he willed everything to his nieces and nephews: Ramona, Richard, Robert, Stephen, and Patti. My brother, Wayne, the executor, was in charge of selling the farm, but many preparations had to be made first. I had the summer to help Wayne sort things out, and Pattie joined me for the month of sorting. Floyd hadn't changed things, and so it was a walk down memory lane finding a horse harness in the loft of the barn, Mum's gardening pants in the closet, and even a wooden leg under a bench. I remembered that Dad had been the executor for a single neighbor when he died, and I guess he just didn't know what to do with Old Bob's wooden leg, so it got thrown under the old tool bench. You never knew what you would find in those days. Many memories! My suggestion to everyone, including myself after this experience, is to regularly downsize and get rid of anything not used. Remember, it's just stuff! Someone will have to sort through it when you are gone, so it is better to do a little at a time.

Edith & Floyd Spicer

The farm

On June 14th, 2015, friends and family joined together at the Crane Valley cemetery for an internment ceremony to bury Mum's and Floyd's ashes. Afterwards, everyone went back to Floyd's shop for a barbeque to reminisce about Mum's and Floyd's lives. For a couple of nights there were thirteen of us bunking together in the old farmhouse. We relished remembering earlier times of us all being together. Just as I had a year ago with my own home, I once again experienced family and friends working together to sort through a lifetime of possessions. In one month, the farm was ready for sale. Seventy-seven years of farming for my parents and brothers was over. A new chapter was about to begin.

The summer is over and it's just about time to go back to school, but first Rob, Calla, and I booked a seven-day cruise to Alaska. Even though it was the second week of September, it was very cold, so there was no sitting out on the deck. What a spectacle it was when we witnessed an ice berg calving! A huge piece of ice detached from the glacier and plunged into the cold, blue-green ocean with a deep rumbled and a swoosh as it slid into the water. It was a great opportunity to continue enjoying Rob and Calla's company and friendship. We would take in an evening show together in the theatre and then I would retire for the night while Rob and Calla went off to enjoy an evening of dancing.

～

Capernwray Bible School – Year 2

Surrender your anxiety! Be silent and stop
your striving and you will see that I am God.
*~ **Psalm 46:10***

Once we were back on dry land, it was time to get ready again for school and meet trudy in Chemainus for the ferry crossing. When trudy and I checked in, we found that we had adjoining rooms above the dining hall with a bathroom between us. I had been given the chance to have my old room back, which I jumped at. I enjoyed this little room with a view of a cherry tree and the ocean. What a blessing. After the busyness of the summer, I felt a deep peace here.

Here I was back on this beautiful island of Thetis for another year of school. I could hardly believe it, but this year I knew what I was getting myself into. There were lectures every morning, many of the same teachers, and the same books of the bible. I was much more relaxed this year and ready to take in all that God had in store for me.

Our very first weekend involved team initiative. Everyone was broken up into teams to work together on completing the initiative course. Trudy and I did not feel that we could physically complete the tasks at our age. We quickly realized that we were not up to climbing a pole and putting a tire over the top, even with a team helping us. Asking Chris Fordham if we could be the cheering section, he quickly said, "Go for it!" So, we cheered with gusto! The staff were so considerate of our age during the whole year. No task was too difficult for us, and when traveling, we were always given a hotel room instead of a sleeping bag on the floor.

During the year, there were many activities that we were involved in. One of the activities was Mission Fest at the Pan Am convention centre in Vancouver. Mission Fest is a three-day event bringing in thousands of people to hear speakers from world-wide mission organizations and to shop various vendor booths. It was a very busy, bustling place to be after the peace and quiet of Thetis Island. The bulk of the students in their twenties slept in sleeping bags on the floor of a church while trudy and I were privileged to have a hotel room in the Pan Am convention centre because of our age. What a blessing that was! Age does have some advantages. We got to experience speakers from all over the world, meander through the multitude of booths, and meet new people. It was a very rewarding but exhausting weekend.

A day in the life of Capernwray started with me being the first to shower and prepare for the day. Breakfast was a 7:45 a.m. While some looked forward to box cereal day, my favourite breakfast was when they made a real treat of baked oatmeal. Those who had morning chores cleaned up after breakfast or chopped veggies for lunch platters. Then, we all headed up to the lecture hall for a short devotional. We had a break time mid-morning and then it was time for the main speaker of the day to present one book of the bible, which we would study that week. Each week was a different book of the bible, and at the end of the week, we had to write up and hand in a journal of what we learned that week. It was a challenge for someone who hadn't been in school for many years, but trudy helped me to learn to use my new computer to complete my journals.

Everyone always looked forward to heading back to the dining hall at noon for lunch. The kitchen always prepared hearty homemade soup, platters of fresh cut veggies, and homemade bread.

After lunch was my time to wash however many pails of eggs were collected from the chickens on the property. One day, after a four-day break, there were nine pails of eggs to clean and stack in egg cartons. I asked Becky, "What are we going to do with all these eggs, Becky?"

"We will have an egg washing bee," she said. The next thing I knew, there were eight of us gathered around the table at the end of the dining room washing eggs. We chatted our time away. While enjoying each other's company, we were finished in one hour with sixty-four dozen eggs, all stacked in the big walk-in refrigerator. Students and staff always had a ready and willing attitude to help one another in the chores. What a joy they were! Our afternoons were our free time to catch up on journals, enjoy the sunshine or have a nap, which I needed every day so I was ready for the lectures in the evening.

Dinner was at 5:45 p.m. and then we all trooped up to the lecture hall for the evening lecture at 7:15 p.m. After evening lectures, there were many activities to keep twenty-year-olds active. The students always invited trudy and I to join them at campfire, floor hockey, or volleyball games. We always thanked them but we were ready for a tea and a quiet snack in our rooms to prepare for the next day. At seventy-one, we just didn't have the energy or stamina for evening activity. It was a very busy time and our nine months of school flew by.

Soon the year was over, and it was time for another graduation ceremony with the cherry blossoms outside my window in full bloom. This time, trudy and I graduated together. Graduation was over… no home to go to… what was next? Both of us were homeless, and we considered what the next chapter of our lives would look like. Do we go to the mission field, rent an apartment in Victoria or Nanaimo? We didn't know.

Rita & trudy 1st day of school

All the student body

Team Initiative cheering section

Team Initiative

Temple Tours

Rita the egg lady

Ferry ride home from school

You are never too old – Bev, Star, Rita & trudy

I got the opportunity to rent a furnished apartment in the same building as trudy in Victoria, to give me time to figure out what the next chapter in my life would look like. I signed up for some drawing classes, a water colour painting class, and just enjoyed the sights of Victoria while I mulled things over. I discovered that God just wanted me to enjoy and experience what He put in front of me. Sometimes it was painting a picture, or listening to a friend who was struggling, or enjoying watching a doe and her fawn grazing the grass. As I surrendered each day to Him, I anticipated whatever surprise He had for me. It was new every day!

Upon getting settled in Victoria, I went to a chiropractor about my back problem. I thought it was my hip that was the problem, but it turned out to be a problem with my back. No one in Alberta had diagnosed it. The chiropractor gave me one treatment to ease the pain but said he wanted me to have an X-ray before treating me further. To be told after the X-ray that I had scoliosis at seventy-three was a shocker. Wasn't that a child's problem? He told me that if I didn't do something about it, I would end up in a wheelchair. That got my attention! Now I wear a full, customized body brace every night and a lift in my right shoe to correct the problem. No more cute shoes I enjoyed all my life! But I thank God that I am not in a wheelchair or having to take pain medication. I thank God for finding this chiropractor in time to stop the progression of this condition.

$\sim$

Finding a New Home

Like a bird that has fallen from its nest
is the one who is dislodged from his home.
*~ **Proverbs 27:8***

At the end of July 2016, trudy and I were on the ferry one Sunday afternoon on our way to Holiday Bible week at Capernwray. It was a beautiful, sunny afternoon as we stood out on the deck, enjoying the sea breeze. "What are you thinking?" trudy asked. "It feels like we are going home," I replied. I didn't think much of the statement, but the next morning on our way to lecture, trudy suggested we go and look at the real estate board beside the lecture hall. Many times, I'd told trudy of my life-long dream of owning a log home on an island, but I never imagined it would ever happen. I had no intention of owning a house again or living on Thetis Island, but there was one house that drew me. I called the realtor on the island to see if we could have a look. Deb Wilson picked us up Wednesday morning to show us four homes for sale on the island. The first time I walked into the home on Vivian Place, I knew instantly it was the place for me. We continued to look at the three others but they didn't measure up to the first one. I asked my children Rob and Calla if they could come and have a look at it on Thursday, and Friday morning, I put in an offer on the house. By Saturday afternoon I owned a new home on Thetis Island. What a surprise! God answered the life-long desire of my heart for a log house on an island. Wow! It isn't exactly a log house, but it's pretty close. Eagles' nests are in the top of the one-hundred-and-fifty-foot spruce and fir trees that shoot into the sky. Eagles soar in the sky, floating on air currents, while hummingbirds flit around the feeder and the little pond at the front. Sometimes, I see deer families as they graze behind the house. This place is my beautiful and peaceful retreat. God answered my unspoken prayer. I have been here four years now, thoroughly enjoying the peace of this place.

While trudy lived with me for seven weeks during the COVID pandemic, we had much time to talk and explore the possibility of her coming to live with me here on Thetis Island. The invitation had been extended four year ago when I moved into the house, but the timing was just not right. Now with both of us at seventy-seven years old, it seems to be a good time. With similar likes and dislikes, we co-habitat well together and look forward to supporting each other in this chapter of our lives. This book would not have happened if it hadn't been for trudy's computer, her writing skills, and us being together for the extended time during the COVID pandemic. It is a little slice of heaven here on Thetis, and it's good to have a companion of similar faith to share it with.

~

Thetis Island Living

Thetis Island Living

Thetis Island Living

Lining up for the ferry to Chemainus

The Next Generation – my joy!

My two granddaughters and great grandson are the joy of my life and a blessing from God.

Valentina & Gram Rita

Alicia & Hazen Shane (Richard's daughter & grandson)

Hazen Shane & G Gram Rita

Why Did I Become a Christian?

For all have sinned and are in need of the glory of God.
~ Romans 3:23

I knew the stories about Jesus being born in the stable at Christmas time and Him dying on the cross at Easter, but I knew in my own life something was missing. I just didn't measure up. I hadn't murdered anyone or stolen anything, and I had always tried to be a good person. I was a good person… or so I thought. When I listened to that speaker at Christian Women's in 1972, I realized that being a good person was not enough. I wanted a relationship with God, but I didn't know how to get that. The speaker said that Jesus came to us as a baby, and when he grew up, he died on a cross to take away my sins so I could have a relationship with God. What sin? The sin of thinking I was a good person? I was okay in my eyes. Did Adam's original sin cast a shadow on the whole of humanity? I knew I was unable to be a good Mum for my children on my own. I lost my temper with them and was not as patient as I would like to be. I was unable to love or be as patient as I would like to be with Ron also. I was unable to be a good person in my own strength. I didn't measure up! I needed someone to save me from myself. When I accepted Jesus as my saviour, He said my sin was thrown into the deepest ocean with a "no fishing" sign, as Corrie Ten Boom stated. So, I took the plunge and asked Jesus to forgive me for my past and to help me to be a better person. It seemed so simple… and yet it changed my whole outlook on my world and how I interacted with my family. Are you searching for more fulfilment in your life? Are you ready to take the plunge and ask Jesus to fill your life until it is overflowing? My life has been so much fuller since I took that step and became a believer forty-eight years ago.

~

Steps to Become a Believer

A – admit you are a sinner

*There is no one who always does what is right,
no, not even one! ~ **Romans 3:10***

*For sin's meager wages is death, but God's lavish gift is
life eternal, found in your union with our Lord Jesus,
the Anointed One. ~ **Romans 6:23***

B – believe Jesus is Lord

*For if you publicly declare with your mouth that Jesus is
Lord and believe in you heart that God raised him from
the dead, you will experience salvation. ~ **Romans 10:9***

C – call upon His name

Everyone who calls on the name of the Lord
will be rescued and experience new life.
~ Romans 10:13

My Prayer for You

I pray that the light of God will illuminate the eyes of
your imagination, flooding you with light, until you
experience the full revelation of the hope of his calling.
~ Ephesians 1:18

✟✟✟

I hear the Lord saying, I will stay close to you, instructing
and guiding you along the pathway for your life. I will
advise you along the way and lead you forth with my
eyes as your guide. So don't make it difficult; don't be
stubborn when I take you where you've not been before.
Don't make me tug you and pull you along. Just come
with me! So my conclusion is this: Many are the sorrows
and frustrations of those who don't come clean with
God. But when you trust in the Lord for forgiveness, his
wrap-around love will surround you.
So celebrate the goodness of God.
~ Psalm 32:8-10

✟✟✟

Endnotes

[1] Used with permission of Doug Harvey from his book on the genealogy of the Spicer family

[2] Used with permission of the Parrsborough Shore Historical Society and included in the book by Doug Harvey

[3] Used with permission of Doug Harvey from his book on the genealogy of the Spicer family written in the first person by Gordon Whitwell Spicer

[4] Used with permission of Laura Livingstone from her thesis on Grass Roots

[5] Bibliography: Canadian Family Tree – Corpus Information 197; Freisen, Gerald – The Canadian Prairies Toronto: University of Toronto Press 1984; Robertson, Heather – Grass Roots Toronto, James Lewis & Samuel 1973

We will always be friends till we are old and senile… Then we can be new friends.